HIS HAND IS BIGGER

Andrew Perry

WESTBOW
P R E S S®
A DIVISION OF THOMAS NELSON
& ZONDERVAN

WestBow Press books may be ordered through
booksellers or by contacting:

WestBow Press
A Division of Thomas Nelson & Zondervan
1663 Liberty Drive
Bloomington, IN 47403
www.westbowpress.com
844-714-3454

ISBN: 979-8-3850-0933-6 (sc)
ISBN: 979-8-3850-0934-3 (e)

Library of Congress Control Number: 2023919123

Print information available on the last page.

WestBow Press rev. date: 10/30/2023

Recently my pastor told a story. It was an old story, one I had heard before, but I rather liked his version of it. It is a kind of modern day parable. An earthly story with a heavenly application. As I was reminded of this old allegory it made me think of the events that occurred in my life, and that of my wife, Thanksgiving weekend 2018. His application was the exact thing I learned that weekend. An eternal truth that now echos with relevance every day of my life.

A young mother took her young son to a store downtown. The store keeper was a kind older gentleman with grandchildren. The young boy knew the storekeeper kept a jar of wrapped hard candy on the counter. He also knew the kind man would occasionally give the candy away. So he walked to the counter and stared at the jar as his mother prepared to pay.

The storekeeper noticed the boy's stare as he slid the jar towards him.

"Take a hand full of candy," he said to the boy.

But the boy just stood there and stared. This surprised his mother who never knew her son to be shy.

"Don't you want some candy?" the shopkeeper asked.

But still the boy stood motionless. So the shopkeeper reached into the jar for the boy and grabbed a hand full of candy and handed it to the boy's mother. The mother put the candy in her purse as she shook her head at her son. After telling her boy to say thank you, they left the shop.

As they walked to the car the mother turned to her son and asked, "You're not usually shy, especially when it comes to candy. Why wouldn't you reach your hand in and take the candy?"

The boy answered, "I wanted the candy. But I knew his hand is bigger than mine."

PRELUDE

Thanksgiving 2018, my wife Jane and I were spending the day at the home of my brother and his wife. Joining us was one of their daughters and four of her girls. It was a relaxing and enjoyable day of visiting that culminated with a traditional Thanksgiving Day meal. Before prayer and eating we each in turn spoke of something for which we were thankful. I don't remember what I said I was thankful for on that day. There were so many things I could have said I suppose. A few months earlier Jane had been to her doctor to get a screening for a lung disease called pulmonary fibrosis. Her mother had died from it as well as several other family members. Family members on both her mother and father's side. So getting tested for it at age 60 seemed prudent. Her scans showed two small spots on her lungs that the lung specialist believed could be PF. He wanted Jane to have a high definition scan that would tell him for sure if it was PF and if so, he would start her treatment for the disease. However, our insurance would not cover the cost of a second scan for three months. The specialist said it wasn't so urgent that we couldn't wait the three months. So that's what we were doing, we were waiting. The doctor had said if it was PF it was very early, he wasn't too worried. That Thanksgiving day one of the many things I was thankful for was the fact that if it was the disease it was early and treatable. I don't know if I said that on that day, but I was thankful for it and prayed the treatment would work and Jane would have a long life. At approximately 6 p.m. we left our brother's house and drove home where we planned an early night. The next day was Black Friday and we both worked retail so we knew we'd have a busy day ahead of us. We slept well that night, anticipating a busy weekend.

BLACK FRIDAY

"When my life was ebbing away, I remembered you, Lord, and my prayer rose to you, to your holy temple." Jonah 2:7

FRIDAY, NOVEMBER 23

We both worked the closing shift on that Friday. Jane was working at the local mall and her shift ended at 10 p.m. I managed two stores and was closing the one furthest away, about a 30 minute drive from our house. It was in a mall that hadn't done very well in the last few years so the mall management had decided to change the closing time from 9 p.m. to 8 p.m. However, since it was Black Friday the hours were extended, but only by an hour. The mall would be closing at 9 p.m. this year, only an extra hour of extended shopping. As far as I was concerned this was good news, I didn't feel being open any later would show any significant increase in sales.

It would be months before I would begin to see, to understand, all the cogs in God's perfect wheel as they rotated into place. I left the mall at 9:30 p.m. unaware that His plan was already in motion as the night unfolded before me.

10:05 p.m.

I arrived home and took Teddy and Annie, our two greyhounds for a walk. It was a short walk since they were anxious for their dinner which was already very late. Ten minutes later I was back in the house and feeding them. I then open a pack of one of those frozen meals with pasta, vegetables and chicken for myself and began heating it in a pan on the stove.

10:33 p.m.

My late dinner was almost done when Jane came through the front door. Our kitchen is on the front of the house so I was close enough to be able to talk to her as she came in. "How was your day?" I asked as our greys greeted her. "Busy," she replied as she gave attention to Teddy and Annie. After an ample amount of pets and kisses were given to the pups she took off her coat and hung it on the coat rack. "How are you feeling?" I asked. "Tired and sore," she replied.

That was the last thing she said before I hear what I thought was a mild groan. I turned and looked into the other room to see Jane laying on the floor. My first thought was that one of the dogs had tripped her or that she had stumbled over one of the shopping bags behind her as she was partly laying on them. I walked to her calling her name, "Jane?" She did not respond. As I knelt next to her and repeated her name I noticed her eyes were open but her face was expressionless. "Are you okay?" I asked. She stared at the ceiling without a reply. I loosened the scarf around her neck and repeated her name. Suddenly she took a gasp of air and stopped breathing. I stood, rushed back to the kitchen, grabbed my cell phone and dialed 911.

10:36 p.m.

For some reason I wasn't panicked. I spoke clear and very matter-of-fact, almost detached from the whole situation. It was like something deep down knew this was how I needed to be so I was just doing what I needed to do. I had already returned to Jane and began to describe her symptoms to the operator. She was not breathing, I told the operator, but then noticed she was taking the same gasp of air about every eight seconds. The lady on the phone instructed me to start doing chest compressions. She counted with me, "one, two, three, four, one, two, three, four."

10:41 p.m.

I suddenly heard sirens and saw flashing lights outside. I told the lady on the phone the ambulance was here. She asked if the door was unlocked and I replied that it was not. She instructed me to go unlock it and then come straight back and continue the compressions. I did as she said though by now I don't recall Jane taking any more gasps of air. Suddenly there was a loud rap at the front door as a man announced, "911" "Come in," I yelled. I then stepped away from my wife letting the paramedics take over. I told them what had happened as I grabbed our curious Grey's and pulled them away. We watched helplessly as one of the men opened a bag valve mask and put on her. Another one began quizzing me about any medications she was on. Due to the tight turn from the rail on our front porch into the house, the ambulance gurney could not be used. A canvas one was brought in and as the men moved her onto it one of the paramedics placed his bag on the stretcher with her. "My bag weighs more than she does," the man said. My petite wife weighed, at most, 105 pounds. They carried her out and one of the men told me where they were taking her. It was the local hospital only a few miles away. After the last man left I watched outside the front window. The ambulance sat unmoving. I watched as the minutes seemed to slow. Were they securing her on the stretcher? Why weren't they moving. What was happening? Would I see the lights turn off? Would one of the EMT's reemerge and come knock on the door? "I'm sorry, we did all we could." But then, after a few more minutes, the ambulance pulled away, lights still flashing.

I turned and looked back into the kitchen, the now empty house (except for me and our two greys). Little pieces of trash scattered on the floor from the freshly opened breathing mask and other items. "Now what?" I thought. "I have to let her family know." Her parents were no longer living and her sister had recently gotten a new number which wasn't in my phone. In fact, I only had the phone number of one of her cousins on my phone.

10:54 p.m.

I sent a text to Beth her cousin, "Pray, Jane collapsed. On way to hospital." I knew Beth would contact other family members for prayers. She sent a text back a few minutes later, then she called and I explained what had happened. After that I then made sure the burner on the stove was turned off, got in my van and drove to the hospital.

I don't know what I expected when I arrived at the hospital's emergency waiting room. But I went in and told the security guard behind the long counter who I was and who my wife was. He told me to have a seat and someone would call for me. I looked around the large waiting area. There seemed like there were a lot of people there, but I managed to find a somewhat secluded spot and sat on a padded bench. I didn't want to talk to anyone, just a doctor or nurse who knew something about my wife. I didn't want to be social with the others waiting there. One of them may ask why I was there, who I was waiting for and I wasn't sure I could say without getting emotional. So far I had held it together and I felt I needed to continue to be able to do that. I sat and I prayed as the minutes ticked by. The bench I sat on was right across from a security guards small desk, which sat right next to a set of double doors leading down a long corridor with rooms on each side of the hallway. I sat numbly watching the man drink his soda. That must be a boring job I thought. The minutes continued to click by. Every now and then a woman would come out and call someone's name and that person would follow her back through the double doors. I watched the time as the minutes turned to thirty minutes, then sixty minutes. The nurses kept coming out from time to time calling a name, but none of those names were mine. As I sat I felt like I was paralyzed, like I was sitting in a shell unable to move, unable to feel. Just numb. I would pray a while, then my thoughts would go elsewhere. Just over 40 years ago my father had collapsed in our living room in the house I had grown up in. It was early morning and I was still in bed. I was awaken by the voice of my mother frantically calling my name. I rushed downstairs to find my father on the floor by the front door, my mother unable to lift him. I tried to lift him too but for some reason I was unable to do so. I remember crying out, "Lord give me the strength." Then I was able to pick up my father, who had suddenly become light as a baby, and carry him to his bed. We had placed a twin bed in the living room for him because after a heart attack he was unable to climb the stairs to his bedroom. As I laid him on the bed and then call for an ambulance I noticed his breathing. He would take a gasp of air about every eight seconds. It was exactly the same thing Jane was doing that night. And, just like my wife, after a few minutes he stopped breathing. They said it was a stroke. I watched my father die that day and now, so many years later, I watched my wife go through the same thing. It was a very bad déjà vu.

I knew Jane was alive when she left in the ambulance but whether she had died on the way to the hospital or after she got there I did not know. No one was coming for me, the nurses were not calling my name. Were they reluctant? Were they talking among themselves, "It's your turn to tell the husband his wife didn't make it." "No we'll wait for the doctor, he'll tell the husband."

A woman, one of the people waiting in that big room, walked over to me. She stood next to my bench just to my right. She reached up and was doing something over my head, I couldn't imagine what. But I was still in a state of numbness, feeling unable to move. I didn't look up to see what she was doing. I didn't slide over to give her more room. I simply sat still, staring out of my shell, wondering why she was standing there. Wondering if the guard was going to get another soda after finishing his first one. Wondering how much longer I'd have to wait. Wondering how the doctor would choose his words to me. Wondering what my reaction would be. Praying again. All the while sitting inside an immovable shell.

Finally the woman walked away. I checked the time

again. The 60 minutes I had been waiting had turned to 75 minutes but it seemed like hours. What if the message that I was waiting hadn't been related to the doctor? That thought temporarily broke me free of my shell and I went back to the long counter to make sure they knew I was there. They did. Someone would come get me as soon as they could, but that was all they could tell me. "No news was good news," I tried to tell myself. I walked back to my bench. The security guard at the small desk watched me. He must have been wondering if I was ever going to move. I looked at the wall behind the bench before I sat down. There was a free cell phone charging port in the wall. At least now I knew what that lady was doing while she was standing over me. She probably wondered if I was ever going to move too. I sat back down and began to pray again.

DARK SATURDAY

". . . I did not understand, things too wonderful for me to know." Job 42:3b

SATURDAY, NOVEMBER 24

12:38 a.m.

The double doors opened again. This time the nurse called my name as her eyes scanned the room. I stood and she looked at me. "Mr. Perry?" she questioned. I nodded. "Come with me," she replied.

As we walked she explained that my wife was currently stable. The doctor would explain more she said. She also warned me that she was not yet awake, was hooked-up to some IV's and that there was a breathing tube going down her throat. I assume she didn't want me to be startled when I saw her. She then walked me into a large area with several side rooms and then into one of those rooms. Jane lay on a bed, her eyes closed and the IV's and tube just as the nurse had described. I felt very little. I was still numb.

It was more like watching a dream or a movie of someone else's life.

I don't remember how long I waited before a doctor spoke to me or maybe he was in the room when I walked in. He said there was a lot of blood on her brain. They had taken a scan or an x-ray, I don't remember what, and that there was a lot of blood. He guessed it was a ruptured aneurysm. He also said that they were not equipped to meet her needs. She would need to be air lifted to Johns Hopkins some 70 miles away. Time was of the essence. But we would have to wait a bit while they arranged everything.

I remember sitting there next to my wife, praying, then talking to her. I didn't know if she could hear me but if she could I tried to stay calm and let her know she was going to be okay. Something I really didn't know myself. I watched the doctors and nurses busying about just outside the room. The doctor was on the phone for a while, then he returned to let me know that Johns Hopkins had no available rooms. They were trying to arrange transport to the University of Maryland Medical Center. He left and I looked at the clock on the wall, then at my wife. "Time was of the essence," I thought remembering the doctor's words. I talked to Jane some more, prayed some more.

12:44 a.m.

I sent another text to her cousin, updating her on what I knew. I kept watching the clock as the minutes ticked by.

12:48 a.m.

Finally the doctor returned. UMMC could take her he told me. I breathed a sigh of relief. He then said they were arranging to have a medevac helicopter take her by air. After he left the room I looked back at my wife as I prayed, "Lord don't let it take long."

12:55 a.m.

The doctor returned to inform me that a coming ice storm had grounded the helicopter and they would have to send an ambulance to come get her. They should be here in an hour or two. My heart sank. The time it would take them to get to Hagerstown, to get her into the ambulance, then drive back to Baltimore and get her into the hospital. It would be hours. Hours! Time is of the essence. The doctor's words echoed in my mind. I looked at Jane again and clenched my teeth to hold it together. "You'll be okay," I told her. "They're going to take you to Baltimore." I prayed again as I watched the clock.

1:13 a.m.

I sent a text to Jane's niece Connie. "Jane collapsed we are at the hospital." I had forgotten to text her earlier, I don't know why. I think I had forgotten her number was in my phone.

1:45 a.m.

The ambulance from UMMC arrived. Three paramedics and a stretcher entered the room. They were calm and reassuring. One of the paramedics told me where they were taking her and asked if I knew the place. I did not, but I had a GPS. "I'll write down the address," she said. Then after a failed attempt to find pen and paper, she wrote it on a paper towel with a black marker - 22 South Greene St. "You can park right on the street," she said. One of the guys with her said, "No, you better park in the deck the next street down." I nodded. "You go ahead," the woman said to me. But before I left she added, "And take your time. It will be a while before you'll be able to see her again anyway." I tried to reassure Jane one last time and told her I loved her before I left.

I drove home, checked on our greys and took them to the backyard for a quick break. I then put my now cold meal in the fridge, I didn't want to eat anyway. Next I grabbed any prescription pills Jane was taking and put them in a bag along with her cell phone. I didn't know if any of what had happened could have anything to do with a drug interaction but I wanted to have them available in case a doctor asked as the paramedics had. Then I changed my clothes and headed for Baltimore.

2:24 a.m.

A lot of things ran through my mind as I drove. None of the doctors or nurses told me not to worry. No one said she was going to be okay. I thought of my father and his death. I wondered if the inevitable was just being delayed. I tried not to think of my life without my wife, my love, my best friend. I thought of other men and how they sometimes said critical things about their wives to each other. I never did. My wife was no more perfect than I was, but after more than 30 years of marriage we were still very much in love. We still held hands in public, still hugged, still kissed each other good bye. And always, always said I love you. Every day we said it. I knew our relationship wasn't perfect. I knew I wasn't the perfect husband. But there wasn't a single person in the whole world I'd rather spend a Saturday with. I wanted to be strong. I didn't want my wife to wake up and see a teary husband. I wanted her to see a smiling confident man, a man that would reassure her that everything was going to be okay. I told myself to stop being selfish, stop feeling sorry for myself. This wasn't about me, about what I had to lose. It was about Jane and what she was going through, what she had to lose. At that my thoughts suddenly stopped. They turned on a tangent I wasn't expecting. What she had to lose? Her life. But she was a believer. She had trusted Jesus as her Savior. Think of what she has to gain. No more sorrow. No more pain. No more worry. She'll see Jesus face to face. Then an image of my wife standing before her Savior came to my mind. I imagined her standing there just looking at him. I imagined him, smiling at her and saying welcome home. What a beautiful thing. I felt overwhelming happiness for my wife and for the first time tears began to swell in my eyes. But not of sorrow or loss, tears of joy for the woman I loved. How much better off she would be in the arms of Jesus than in the arms of a fallible husband. Was I really being selfish wanting her to live? I found myself struggling with that question. I wasn't ready to lose my wife, not now, not yet. "Lord I know I'm being selfish, but I want her to live. I want my baby back."

3:41 a.m.

I arrived at the hospital and parked in the underground deck then walked a block back to the main entrance on 22 Greene Street. It was a large building taking up a full city block or more. I entered the large revolving door and was directed to the security desk. I told them who I was there to see. The security guard looked up my wife's name. She then told me where she was as she wrote the room number on a color-coded bracelet and placed it on my arm. She asked if I knew where it was. When I told her that I did not she gave me directions and said if I got lost just show my bracelet to a staff member and they should be able to help me. I don't recall the room or even the floor I was sent to, just that it was near the back of the hospital and several flights up. When I arrived at the unit a set of double doors requiring a pass card stood before me. A sign indicated a button to push for admittance. I noticed there was what looked like a camera above the button as I pressed it. After a few moments the door opened and I walked through. I found myself in another hall and looking to my left I saw a nurse station with two or three nurses standing there. I walked to them and gave them my wife's name. The nurse at the desk looked her up on the computer and told me she was still in surgery. She said they were draining the blood on her brain and it may be a while yet. She said I could wait in one of the waiting areas just outside the double doors I had just come through. She would let the doctors know I was there. I thanked them and went back out. I found two waiting rooms just outside the doors. They were small and one seemed a little darker and maybe a bit more formal than the other, I chose that one to wait in. I sat the bag with my wife's pills next to me along with my rain jacket. As I waited I prayed some more and tried not to let all the things that had run through my head buff at me. I read every sign in that room at least three times, maybe more. I don't remember how long I waited before the first person came out to see me. It was a woman doctor or nurse or nurse practitioner I don't recall which. She confirmed that my wife had had a ruptured aneurysm and that they were draining the blood from her brain. She also explained that she would soon be transferred to another wing of the hospital where a neurosurgeon would perform a coiling procedure. While I remember some of what she told me the only thing I remember verbatim was, "There was a lot of blood on her brain." Her eyes widened as she repeated, "a lot of blood," emphasizing "a lot." She said someone would come get me when they were ready to move her. Then I was left alone though for how long I don't remember. Minutes, hours, all I could do was to wait and pray. It was now the very early hours of Saturday morning and I didn't want to wake any family members by calling or texting them.

In time a young man came out to talk to me. He didn't know if anyone had spoken to me or not so he explained again about the aneurysm. He even took out his cell phone and did a search for it to show me some animated graphics so I could better understand. He also told me that the procedure to put the drain in my wife's head had gone well, but it would take some time to fully drain. He then asked me to sign some papers and left promising to return when they were ready to move my wife. I don't remember how long he was gone but when he returned I asked if I would be able to see her. He told me they were taking her to surgery for the coiling procedure and that I should be able to see her in recovery after that. He showed me another graphic on his cell phone of what a coiling was. I saw that a thin wire would be run in a vein up through her leg and all the way to her brain. The aneurysm was like a small balloon on the side of a blood vessel. The balloon had burst and blood had flowed into the space between Jane's brain and skull causing her to pass out. And though he didn't say, I assumed it also caused her to stop breathing. He also informed me that the aneurysm was in a bad place. It was at the base of her skull right where a main artery forked. The aneurysm had formed right at the fork. He continued to explain that the doctor would be inserting a wire into the aneurysm making it coil-up and stopping more blood from entering the aneurysm. The surgeon who was to perform the procedure was just coming on his shift and the young man was going to take me to talk to him before he got started.

7:46 a.m.

It was a long walk to meet the surgeon, we went down an elevator, across a long hall, up another elevator, and down more halls till I was asked to wait in a hall overlooking an indoor courtyard several floors down. As I waited for the man to return I walked to the rail and looked out across the courtyard. I was five or six flights up and through the glass corridors across from me I saw nothing but empty hallways. It was the early hours of a holiday weekend and it seemed that that busy hospital was not so busy right at that moment. There was nothing but silence as I stood alone waiting, staring at nothing in particular. But then something caught my eye. I saw through the glass rail several floors below me a lone woman in a hospital bed being wheeled along. There were multiple tubes running into her. Her head was half shaved and a brownish color splashed the top of her head and part of her face. She did not look good, even at that distance. I stood and watched until my wife was wheeled out of sight. It seemed like a surreal moment. That I should have walked to that rail at the very moment when my wife was passing by. That I should by chance see her as I had never seen her before, like no husband would ever want to see his wife. The numbness I was feeling before had returned. Like a self defense mechanism it wasn't allowing me to feel. The person I saw was just a person. A patient in a hospital bed. When she had been wheeled out of sight, leaving the corridor empty once more, I continued to stare at the spot. Numb.

Soon the young man came back for me. He would take me to a room, a private area where the surgeon would be talking to me before the procedure. I followed the man once more. This time he took me into a large room or corridor with a long row of beds with curtains as dividers between each bed. In what seemed like another surreal moment the room was dark and the beds were all empty. "He'll be here in a moment," the young man told me as he left me alone in that place. Where was I? I wondered why it was so dark. Why the beds were all empty. Was my lack of sleep, my mental numbness making me feel like I had stepped into the Twilight Zone? No, I reasoned, just a temporarily unused wing of the hospital. Still, it somehow played on the drunk-like numbness I was feeling. But soon my eyes were drawn to a movement coming out of the darkness at the far end of that long room. I watched as a man in a white coat walked toward me. He looked to be in his fifties and something in his walk, something in his face made me feel he was a humble man. As he reached me he put out his hand, "I am Doctor Mason Gainer," he said. He invited me to walk with him as he explained what had happened to my wife and the coiling procedure he planned to do. He wanted me to understand that it was not without risk and that with the amount of blood that had flooded my wife's brain, that her recovery was uncertain. However, he also wanted to reassure me that he had done the procedure many times. Dr. Gainer was a kind, unassuming man and before he left me he directed me to an indoor garden area where I could wait as the approximately three hour procedure was performed.

Then, as he turned from me to start up a flight of steps, I said one last thing to him. "I'm sure you will, but take good care of my wife. She's my baby." I think I wanted to say more to the man who was about to perform a life saving procedure on my wife, but that was all I managed. Dr. Gainer nodded and continued up the steps. I headed for the garden waiting area.

8:06 a.m.

The garden sat on the protruding third floor of a seven story atrium with a beautiful skylight roof. Obviously intended to be a relaxing atmosphere for anxiously waiting family members. Among plants and small trees it featured couches, tables and chairs. There weren't many people there at this early hour. I didn't want to talk to anyone and finding a secluded spot was easy. I took out my cell phone to send some more texts. It was Black Friday weekend and I had to let people know I wasn't coming in. I prayed some more, then laid down on one of the couches and tried to sleep a little, but it was useless, I wasn't going to sleep. I sat back up and after a bit I heard someone call my name.

Dr. Lynn, a neurosurgeon that worked with Dr. Gainer, had come to explain the procedure to me. She did not know whether anyone had talked to me about it and wanted to make sure I had been informed. She spoke very positive and told me that Dr. Gainer was the best neurosurgeon they had. Maybe even the best there was. I was thankful for this. She confirmed the information I had given earlier and left me.

I don't know how long I waited before I got up and left. I just walked out of the hospital. I needed air, needed to walk, I m not sure what.

10:26 a.m.

I wasn't even near the hospital when my phone rang. It was Dr. Gainer. He apologized for calling on the phone but said he was unable to find me in the garden area. I was embarrassed. What kind of husband leaves the hospital when his wife is in surgery? I apologized and said that I was tired and not thinking. That I had left for a bit. He replied that that was fine, not to worry, he just wanted me to know that the procedure had gone well and that my wife was being moved to an ICU for her recovery. I thanked him profusely and apologized again before rushing back to the hospital.

10:47 a.m.

Nurocare ICU West is on the seventh floor of the UMMC building. It is a large unit with around 12 single patient care rooms in a U shape around a nurse's counter and staff break room. A video doorbell is pressed by visitors to gain access. I entered the unit and was directed to my wife's room. The large glass sliding door to her room was open. It was dark with the lights on low. Jane's head, still stained from the iodine solution, was half shaved and bandaged. A tube ran from under the bandage on her head into a sack filling with red liquid (which I would later learn was a mixture of blood and brain -or spinal- fluid). Two tubes ran down her throat and there were no less than six needles in her arms. Her eyes were closed as she rested. My very first thought was "she's beautiful." Even laying there like that in that hospital bed, Jane was still the most beautiful woman I knew. The nurse asked if I was her husband which I confirmed. "She's still coming out of her anesthesia," she explained. I spoke to Jane to let her know I was there. I wasn't sure how much she understood. Then a doctor came in and began to test her reflexes. They were not good. He said her name loudly. Her eyes opened in a groggy state and closed again. He called her again and got the same response. He pinched her left hand and she pulled it away, her right hand but she didn't respond. He then tried her feet. There was a slight movement of her left leg, but no more. He then introduced himself to me as Jim. After making sure I understood her procedure he said he would be back to check on her later. He was sure of getting a better response from her as she became more awake. I had been so focused on praying for her to just survive I had forgotten about the possibility she could have brain damage. But I was thinking about it now. She could be partly paralyzed. She may need to relearn things, how to walk, how to speak. There was no way of knowing what damage there was until she was fully awake. The nurse said that the effects of the anesthesia should wear off in a few hours. All I could do was wait and see.

Jane was mostly sleeping now so I decided to try to eat something. It was now late morning on Saturday and I hadn't eaten anything since a late lunch on Friday. I went to a coffee shop downstairs and forced myself to eat a pre-made breakfast sandwich and drink a coffee. I prayed some more as I sat alone at the table. I then tossed my half eaten sandwich in the trash and went back to Jane's room.

11:12 a.m.

The nurses, doctors and staff were all very nice in the ICU. While their focus was on my wife they also asked if I needed anything. Although awake, Jane continued in a dream like state. The nurse tried to reassure me that it would take time for her to fully wake.

11:52 a.m.

The next test the doctor did was the same as the last. Pinching her hands and feet to see if she would pull away. She pulled away her left hand when pinched and moved both her feet. Her right hand, however, showed no response. As the doctor spoke to her she would look at him but was unresponsive when he asked her to raise two fingers or squeeze his hand. "I'll check back in an hour," the doctor said. Left alone with her I held her hand. I squeezed it, but her hand was limp in mine. I spoke, she turned her head and looked right at me, but there was no response, no expression, just a blank stare.

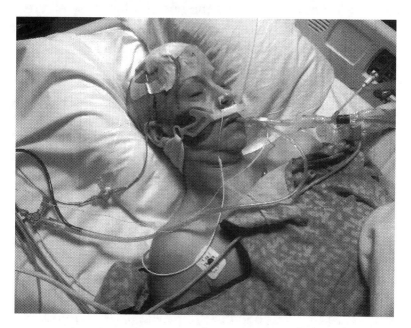

Jane, day one in the ICU.

12:18 p.m.

A nurse brought in a bottle of liquid which she explained was for her feeding tube. They were very good at explaining what they were doing and why. I told her that it looked like a mocha latte, which was one of Jane's favorite drinks. Levity helped me deal with what was happening. The already pleasant nurse smiled. Every nurse, every doctor and staff member that walked into the room, and there were a lot, were very pleasant, upbeat and encouraging. But as the afternoon wore on Jane's responses were unchanged. Verbal commands held no meaning to her and her right arm was still not responding. I continued to talk to her off and on when she was awake as did the nurses when they entered the room. Jane would turn her head and look at the speaker but remain expressionless. I continued to pray.

4:58 p.m.

Then, finally, on one of the doctor's hourly checks, he pinched her right hand and she pulled it away. I nearly broke out in tears of happiness. I didn't want Jane to see me cry, to worry about me, and it took all I had to hold back. This meant that she was not paralyzed in any part of her body. She had fully functioning limbs, so even if she had to relearn things like how to walk or feed herself, it would be physically possible. The doctor made every effort to keep his expression professional. Perhaps so that I could not tell when a result was good or bad. Maybe it was an effort to keep me from worrying if a result was not good. Or maybe it was just this doctor's way. But he didn't have to show his satisfaction this time, I knew it was a good sign and I thanked the Lord for it.

5:45 p.m.

Visiting hours ended at 6 p.m. according to the sign outside the unit and started again at 8 a.m. Though I didn't know or understand at the time, I didn't have to leave. There was a 90 minute window during the shift change from 6 to 7:30 that no new visitors were allowed in. But thinking I had to leave at 6:00 I prepared to go as the evening approached. It had been well over 9 hours since Jane had gone under and she obviously should be fully awake by this time. However, she still was not responding to questions or commands. She was as awake as she was going to be but gave no more than blank stares.

6:00 p.m.

It was time for me to go. I took Jane's hand in mine and held it tight. With IV's running into her, tubes in her mouth and a tube in her head, I looked into those beautiful eyes as she stared back at me. I moved my face close to hers and said, "I love you." Her expression was unchanged. The nurse tried to reassure me that she may still be a bit foggy, that she may be better tomorrow. But I could tell from her expression that she didn't believe her own words. Jane was fully awake. And while she reacted to negative stimuli, her cognitive ability was minimal. She was in a type of vegetative state. I would later find one medical site's definition in part as "an absence of responsiveness and awareness. Some may have complex reflexes, including eye movements, yawning, and involuntary movements to noxious stimuli, but show no awareness of self or environment."

I left the room that night realizing that my wife was in a vegetative mental state. She could move her arms and legs and look at people but there was no understanding. She didn't know me and perhaps never would again.

When I left the hospital that night I was wearing a heavy winter coat and carried a book bag with some miscellaneous things from home. I had not checked the weather forecast and found myself walking to the parking deck in a heavy rain. I had put the bag under my coat and zipped it up hugging it in place as I walked. As the pouring rain drenched me, I couldn't help thinking how Jane would scold me for not having a rain coat or an umbrella. I forced myself to keep walking, to not let my emotions get the best of me. I didn't want to lose it outside the hospital in the pouring rain. I managed to hold it together and made it to my van in a lower level of the deck. I sat alone and drenched in my van in that dark underground concrete structure. I took a breath and decided to call my older brother Tommy, to update him on Jane's condition so he would know how to pray. I did well at first explaining how the day had gone. But then I got to those words. For the first time spoken out loud. "She doesn't know me." That was when I completely lost control. A night and day's worth of penned-up emotion came flooding out of me. I cried and I moaned. My poor brother could only say, "I'm sorry, I'm sorry." I stared at the low ceiling of the deck above me, the rain water had found it's way down and was seeping through from above. I felt like I was drowning as I gasped for air. My beautiful loving wife didn't know me and may never again understand those words, I love you. She was lost to me. Alive, yes, but dead to any knowledge of me, of our lives together, of her family, her friends. Sixty years of life. It was all gone. All lost in a moment. I was overwhelmed with emotions I could hold back no more. In hindsight I thank the Lord for having a godly understanding older brother. There wasn't much he could say, but he listened. I finally stopped blubbering and he talked to me a bit. I don't remember now what he said, what I said, but he prayed. He prayed for me and he prayed for Jane. When I hung up I felt a calm come over me. "She's in Your hands now," I prayed, "but she always has been."

I drove home that night with my emotions in check but my mind racing. I had gone from an emotional wreck to "I have to think straight." What next? Would my wife be able to feed herself? Would she be able to take care of herself in any way? In her current state I couldn't see her doing anything for herself. I could take care of her, but for how long? I'd eventually have to go back to work. We would need the insurance, the income. Family could help. But that would be short term. They all had family and jobs too. Her sister lived close by but her health wasn't good. Her niece? Again, she may be able to help a while, but she had a job and kids to take care of. The thought of putting my wife in some kind of medical care home was crushing to think of. And could I even afford that? Would insurance cover it? Would it be temporary or would it need to be long term? Would she know what was going on? Would she get even a little better, would it be just enough to know I had abandoned her to be cared for by strangers? Would she understand? How much time would I be able to spend with her in a medical care home? My mind raced with all these things. Then it would go back to seeing her in that hospital bed and the fact that she no longer knew me. I struggled to push those thoughts from my mind as I drove. I couldn't tear-up while driving.

When I arrived home that night I numbly went through the motions of things I needed to do. Walk the dogs, fix something to eat, clean the kitchen. Then I sat down to my computer to give Jane's family an email update on the events of the last 24 hours. Later I sat in the den with the greys for comfort and looked around the room. Still decorated for fall and Thanksgiving, Jane's touch was everywhere. Not just in the den but the whole house. She loved to decorate and everywhere I looked I was reminded of that part of her. Just one of the many parts of her now lost. She loved making the house a home. I imagined myself leaving everything untouched. I imagined it being the middle of July and still looking like Thanksgiving. A home stuck in time. People would tell me it was unhealthy no doubt. But would I care. Would it give me comfort or pain? Would Jane make it that long? How long do people live after something like this? Would she live a few months in this vegetative state only to die without ever knowing me or anyone else again? I don't remember how long it took me to fall asleep that night but I remember waking up to an early alarm and heading back to Baltimore. I wanted to be there when visiting hours started again at 8 a.m.

THAT YOU MAY BELIEVE SUNDAY

"he stayed where he was . . . 'and for your sake I am glad I was not there, so that you may believe.'" John 11:6b & 15a

SUNDAY, NOVEMBER 24

After my emotional release the day before and then getting at least a few hours of sleep I felt more in control that Sunday morning as I drove to UMMC in Baltimore. I was ready for a serious talk with the Lord. I needed God's help but I also knew that sometimes He wants us to go through things we may not want to go through. I was well aware of the Lord's Prayer. Jesus taught us to pray, "Our Father in heaven, hallowed be your name." (Matt. 6:9b) He started with an acknowledgment of who He was and of His Holiness, a kind of praise. Then, "your kingdom come." (Matt. 6:10a) This welcomes God's future kingdom, a time of no more sorrow or pain. These were all good things. But then came the hard part, "Your will be done." (Matt. 6:10b) Those words echoed in my mind. Thy will be done.

What if it was God's will for Jane to spend the rest of her life in that vegetative state. To never know me again. Or to die. To go to sleep tonight and never wake up. What if that was God's will? Did I really want to ask for God's will to be done knowing it could very well be that. Then I thought, the Bible also teaches us to "present your request to God." (Phil. 4:6b) I knew what I wanted. I wanted my Jane back. I wanted to walk into that room that morning and I wanted her to know me. That was my request. But how could I ask the God of the universe, who I believed truly loved and wanted the best for me, how could I ask Him to do something outside His will - if it was part of God's will for Jane's condition to continue. I was torn. What do I pray? Thy will be done or my will be done? In the end I had to ask myself, do you trust God or do you not trust God? I trust God I answered. Then, I told myself, you know how to pray. So I praised God, took a deep breath and prayed the most difficult prayer of my life. "Lord," I prayed, "you teach us to pray thy will be done. But you also say, let your request be made known. So here it is. My request is that when I walk into that room this morning, Jane will know me. Even if she'll have to relearn things. Even if it takes months of recovery. Even if she never fully recovers, please bring her back to me. Please let her know me." I had to clench my teeth to finish. "But if it is not your will. If it is not your will to bring her back to me, give me the strength to get through it. Lord . . . thy will be done. I trust you."

As hard as it was to pray those words after I had said it, after I had said, "I trust you." I started to feel a calm. I guess I had forgotten the rest of that verse from Philippians chapter four. After telling us to let our request be made known the apostle Paul continued, "And the peace of God, which transcends all understanding, will guard your hearts and your minds in Christ Jesus." (Phil. 4:7) I was experiencing that peace as I drove.

In hindsight I am reminded of the apostle Peter when Jesus bid him to come to him on the water during the storm. At first Peter did well, but then he took his eyes off Jesus and he began to sink. I'm keeping my eyes on you Lord. As I parked in the lower levels of the parking deck and headed to Jane's room my heart began to pound. In a few short minutes I would know. As I walked into the building I almost began to tremble. But then I simply started repeating those words. "I trust you. I trust you." I began feeling calm again as I walked to the glass elevator. I boarded it, pressed the button for the seventh floor and turned to stare at the doors. As the flights ticked away I repeated, "I trust you. I trust you." Then the doors opened and I exited. I walked to the doors of the ICU and pressed the video doorbell and waited. "It doesn't matter what I see when I walk into that room," I thought. "The Lord is with me and through Him I will get through this. We will get through this." The double doors opened and I walked through them without hesitation. "I trust you," I repeated, "I trust you." Then I rounded the nurse's station and froze. There standing right in front of my wife's room was a team of doctors, nurses, and men in suits. Most with open computers sitting on top of little rolling carts, some with pads taking notes, all staring into my wife's room. A flurry of thoughts ran through my mind. I didn't know what this meant, but I figured it was either very good or very bad. My hesitation was short lived as I forced myself forward and repeated one last time, "I trust you." The group in front of my wife's room were talking until they saw me approach and fell silent. I glanced at them, some smiled, some seemed stone faced. I pulled my eyes from them and walked into the room. I saw a nurse busying about my wife who was sitting up in bed. All the tubes and needles from the night before were still attached to her. Her head turned to me as I walked in and as my eyes met hers her face lit-up. She knew me. She knew me! As I walked to her bedside tears of happiness began to flow. I didn't want Jane to see me cry but I could not hold back the tears. With the tubes still in her mouth she was unable to speak but instead gave me a look of concern and worry. I quickly explained that yesterday she didn't know me and I was afraid she would never know me again. Her eyes showed shock and then the sweetest look of concern for me as I finally managed to check my tears. As I hugged my wife the nurse said to me, "You are very lucky, what has happened here is amazing."

The tubes were taken out later that day and her road to recovery continued. She stayed in the ICU for just over two weeks as the blood slowly drained from her head. Her recovery went very well though she went through a short time of regression the doctors attributed to a sleeping medicine they gave her for a day or two. During the two weeks in ICU her memory was not good. At first she would forget things within seconds of telling her, then within minutes and finally she would remember things for several hours. Also, her mind seemed to be, in part, stuck in the late 1980's. While she remembered who was President, she didn't remember family members who had passed. She kept asking why her parents, both no longer living, hadn't been in to see her. I learned of what her doctor called a bell curve recovery. It was possible for her to improve for the first week and then crash the second week. But she did not.

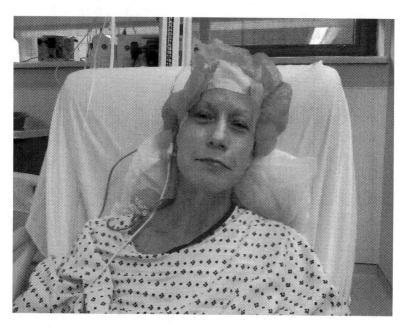

A few days after the tubes came out.

WHAT HAS HAPPENED HERE . . .

"In my distress I called to the Lord, and he answered me. From deep in the realm of the dead I called for help, and you listened to my cry." Jonah 2:2

After just over two weeks she was moved to a local rehab center in our hometown where I could more easily visit and stay longer. Her memory began to improve rapidly then. She began remembering family who had passed away but didn't remember not knowing just a week before. Then, just before Christmas she was sent home. Though still a little weak, mostly from being bed ridden, she was almost fully recovered. Two months later and she was back to work. Then a small setback occurred when a follow-up scan showed the coil that filled the aneurysm had compressed. The doctor had to add coils and a stint but the procedure went well and she was only in the hospital for two days. On the day the procedure was done the doctor, Dr. Gainer, walked me to see Jane as she was being wheeled to recovery. As we walked he suddenly stopped, shook his head and with knotted brows said, "Her recovery . . . the extent of her recovery is amazing. It . . . it just doesn't happen." Dr. Gainer knew the human brain. He knew how it was suppose to work. It was like his world had betrayed him, what was suppose to be wasn't. Someone had flattened his world and he was baffled at how to handle it. My mind went back to that Sunday morning, the first day she awoke and knew me. The doctors and nurses in the ICU seemed to always guard their speech, never over reacting, never sensationalizing. However, I remembered what the nurse had said that morning. Unable to check her own amazement she blurted out, "You are very lucky, what has happened here is amazing." But I knew better. Luck had nothing to do with it. The prayers of God's people had everything to do with it. But it was amazing. It was amazing because we serve an amazing God. And then, as if in conformation, Dr. Gainer was saying that the kind of recovery Jane had experienced, "just doesn't happen." All I can say is that with God, all things are possible. And that He wants us to trust Him because He has a better plan. My plan, my will was that Jane would recover enough to know me and to be able to at least help care for herself. But my plan had limited God. God's plan was for Jane to make a full recovery, more than I dared hope for. When I prayed "Thy will be done" I assumed it would be the harder road. And though it was a hard road, the Lord blessed us more than I had expected. Today I'm glad God did not answer my prayer with my will, but with His will. He had a better plan, a bigger hand. I have learned to trust God no matter what. No matter what.

At the rehab center getting strength back.

BEHIND THE CURTAIN
- GOD'S PLAN

I have learned to kiss the wave that throws
me against the Rock of Ages.

-Charles Spurgeon

In the months that followed I began to understand all the things the Lord had orchestrated as he worked His will. Like a playwright or a composer of a musical suite. Each movement in His masterpiece was planned in advance and executed with perfection, with precision, with intent. And it began months before that night my wife collapsed in our livingroom.

As I mentioned before, my job as a multi-store manager had me traveling between two stores. One was in a shopping center in my hometown, the other was in a mall approximately 30 miles away. The mall store was doing well, though not as well as my hometown store, but the mall itself was not. Most of the stores had closed or moved out. Each month the halls of that once vibrant shopping destination looked more and more as a ghost town. In years past Black Friday hours were extended hours. The mall would open as early as 6 a.m. and stay open as late as midnight or later. However, with a dramatic drop in traffic, the regular closing time had already been changed from 9 p.m. to 8 p.m. It was no surprise then, when the mall management announced that Black Friday's extended hours would only be to 10 p.m. But then, one of the larger stores (known as an anchor store) objected. It seems they did not want to spend the extra payroll for what they felt would be a lack luster evening. So, with less than two months till Black Friday, the extended hours were changed once more. The mall would only be open till 9 p.m. on that most famous of shopping days. That change in the closing time allowed me to be home when Jane walked through the door. An hour or two later and I would have most likely come home to find my wife dead on the floor. God's prelude had begun.

The Lord allowed the aneurysm to burst just after Jane walked through the door. Not while she was driving. Not as she walked from the driveway to the front door. Rather, inside the house, mere steps from where I stood. Within a minute a 911 operator gave CPR instructions that kept life saving blood flowing. Had the aneurysm burst any sooner the outcome could have been very different. God's symphony had begun with perfect timing.

Then there was the long delay in getting the blood drained. She spent hours laying in a hospital bed as blood slowly seeped into her brain. At this point one may think where was God in that. The survival rate from a brain bleed is around 50 percent. If the patient does survive, the possibility of a full recovery lowers significantly as the bleed increases. Studies I have read seem to indicate that most people with severe bleeds will never recover completely. One study stated that just 13% achieved what they called a good functional outcome after six months. But nothing I read stated that anyone with a severe bleed recovers 100%, much less within just a few weeks. So where was God? Was this delay a part of His plan? Did God want my wife to wake-up Saturday morning and be little more than a mental vegetable? I can only answer with a resounding yes! Why did Jesus delay in getting to his friend Lazarus when he knew he was sick. Was he sadistic? Did he want him to die? I believe the answer is no and yes. No, he does not enjoy it when we suffer, but he knows it can lead to a higher purpose, a better outcome ("I consider that our present sufferings are not worth comparing with the glory that will be revealed in us." Romans 8:18). But why would he want Lazarus to die? Jesus said it himself in John 11:15, "and for your sake I am glad I was not there, so that you may believe." Verse 17 goes on to tell us that by the time he came, "he found that Lazarus had already been in the tomb for four days." (John 11:17) I believe that Jesus wanted there to be no mistake, what was about to happen was miraculous. As he said earlier in verse four of the same chapter, "This sickness will not end in death. No, it is for God's glory so that God's Son may be glorified through it." (John 11:4) What an honor he bestows on his friend, that Lazarus would be used to the glory of God, to glorify the Son of God. When Jane lay bleeding for hours without relief, I believe it was so there could be no mistake. Her healing was miraculous. In the words of her nurse that Sunday morning, "Amazing." A healing had taken place that her neurosurgeon said, "just doesn't happen." So were all the full beds at Johns Hopkins unfortunate luck? Was a coming ice storm a misfortune? Was the long wait and long drive bad karma? No, no and no, rather it was just the next part of God's flowing melody.

I believe with all my heart that God honored my wife by allowing her to show the glory of God the Father through Jesus His Son. In short, yes, it was God's will and he was there all the time.

Another outcome from the long delay that hasn't escaped my notice is the fact that the hospital's best neurosurgeon would perform the coiling procedure. Dr. Gainer was just coming on his shift at the hospital as Jane was being prepped. Otherwise, a possibly tired surgeon at the end of a long 12 hour shift may have been performing the procedure. The Grand Maestro's plan continued it's flawless flow.

> "For as Jonah was three days and three nights in the belly of a huge fish, so the Son of Man will be three days and three nights in the heart of the earth."
>
> Matthew 12:40

I hope I am not thinking it a stretch, I do not believe that I am. But I am told that the number three in Hebrew means harmony, new life, and completeness. That the number 3 can point to Jesus. His death, burial and resurrection. He was crucified on a Friday, was in the grave for three days and rose on a Sunday. Jane collapsed on a Friday and was, in a sense, mentally dead for three days before being restored on a Sunday. Like Jonah, I believe this was God's way to further point us to Jesus. His rollicking finale if you will. A final sense of "let there be no doubt, this is from God."

Jane and I have learned an important spiritual lesson about trusting God. But not just us, our family and friends did as well. Family members prayed for her that Friday night and Saturday. We left her in God's hands and prayed His will be done. I realized that my will had limited God, but He had a better plan. For some reason I had assumed God's plan for us was going to be the more difficult road, but it was not. I know that other times His will is that we take a more difficult path, but I have learned that He will always be there for us.

I also realized that when we pray for God's will to be done, we then need to be ready to accept His will. When I prayed, Thy will be done, I was ready to accept His will. Even if it was the harder road. In fact, I expected it to be. I had no idea how I was going to handle it, but I had faith that God would see me through it. However, in His good grace, the harder road was not His will. A year and a half later Jane's cousin Dave lay in a hospital bed with COVID 19. A man who had prayed for Jane as she lay in the ICU fighting for her life. Many of the same people who prayed for Jane and saw her healed, now prayed for Dave. I prayed as I did for Jane, "Please heal him, but above all, Thy will be done." About a week later Dave died in the hospital. Was that God's will? Yes, I believe it was. I believe that with all my heart. But the obvious next question is why? Why did God see fit to heal Jane and not Dave? Was she more deserving? At the time we were not going to church. We had left our last church for various reasons and had not yet found another one. Dave was actively serving in his church. What about the people who prayed for Dave? Were the people who prayed for him less spiritual? The same people who prayed for Jane prayed for Dave. In fact, possibly more believers were praying for him as he belonged to his local church. The why question is not so easily answered. Even if we could say, "all things being equal" —which we in fact can not but if we could, even then, God's plan is different from person to person. Why did God allow Jane to lay for hours in a hospital bed while blood flooded her brain? Because it was part of His plan. In Jane's case the Lord seems to have revealed the reason and we've seen the miraculous outcome. But in Dave's case He has not done this, or at least not to my knowledge. But then, the Lord is not obligated to let us see behind the curtain, so to speak. I think that's why faith is so important. I had complete faith in God when I prayed for Jane that Sunday morning and I'm glad I did. The bottom line is God doesn't always allow us to see His reasons for what He does. But we have to have faith that His will is always better. It may not feel like it at the moment, but if we just trust Him, His symphony, His plan, His will always works for the good. The gospel was presented at Dave's service. Could it be that there was a colleague, a friend, or an acquaintance at that service who needed to hear the gospel? Perhaps this was the only time they would listen to such a message. This life may never reveal the answer. But it's not necessary for us to know. It's only necessary that we have faith in God.

A few months after Jane's recovery the company that I had worked for, a company that had been around for sixty years, and I had worked for for nine years, announced it was going out of business and I would be losing my job. I worried not one single day. I praised the Lord for the opportunity to not only exhibit my faith to him, but to my coworkers as well. My wife and I told several of my peers that we would pray for them to get specific jobs that they had applied for and all of them did, including myself.

Today we get up every morning and go about our business. We go to work, the grocery store, church, take a walk, everything is back to normal. At least it is outwardly. But the grace God has shown us has so increased my faith that I think that I shall never again doubt my God. Some days it is easy to get caught-up in everyday life and forget. Forget the ending our story could have had if not for the grace of God. But then he reminds me. It may be something I hear on the radio as I'm driving, or the words of a song in church. If someone were to catch a glimpse of me at those times they may wonder why my eyes have suddenly swelled with tears. But they are not tears of sadness, rather tears of joy. Tears at being overwhelmed by the love of God and how wondrously he displayed that love in a very personal way to me. But then I realize he's done so before. He sent his only son to die for me. For me personally. Greater love has no man.

POSTSCRIPT

The year before these events happen the Lord began speaking to me and teaching me about prayer and His will. He did this in subtle, yet very definitive ways. Ways that a sceptic might say were mere coincidences. But the fact that these things happened repeatedly and often in close succession would make the odds beyond coincidence. Though I will not go into the details of the events I think God was preparing me, preparing my faith, for what was to come. Those series of events had never happened to me before and has not since. But I thank God for those gentle warm-ups for what was coming. It is my prayer that someone might read this account and find strength and comfort in that fact that He still cares for us.

I am thankful for the people God put in place to care for my wife during this time. From the 911 operator to the paramedics, to the doctors and nurses at our local hospital and UMMC. And of course our friends and family who prayed for Jane. I am also thankful that the high definition scan of Jane's lungs revealed that she did not have PF.

Finally, I am thankful for our new church family and the pastor. After writing this story I did nothing with it for more than two years. Partly because of COVID shut-downs and partly because I wasn't sure what to do with it. It was my pastor's sermons on getting involved and ministering to others that inspired me to do something with the story that lay dormant on my computer. Not my story, not even Jane's story, but God's story. A story of His continued grace in our lives.

Though the names have been changed to protect the privacies of those involved, all other details are the facts to the best of my knowledge and remembrance. This I can state with confidence thanks to a journal I kept during those days and the time stamps on my cell phone.

PICTURES

Teddy visits Jane in the ICU.

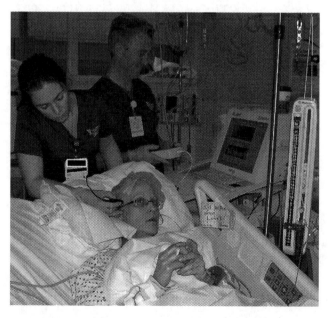

The Doppler ultrasound, just one of the many tests administered during her two week stay in the ICU.

With Jane's memory being so short those first weeks I left a note so she would know I was coming back soon. It included my signature and our life verse (I Cor. 13:8a) on the lap of a teddy bear from home.

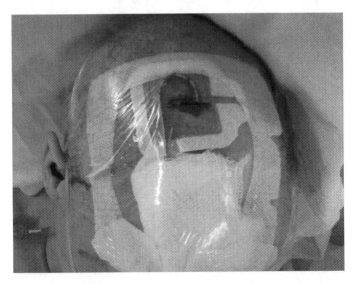

The tube draining the blood from her brain was in till about day 14.

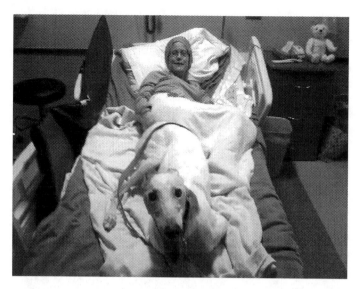

Annie, our other greyhound, got to visit mom in rehab.

Christmas day 2018, 31 days after Black Friday.

IN HIS ARMS

On Sunday, April 16, 2023 at 8:33 p.m. by beautiful wife Jane went to be with the Lord. Her aneurysm re-ruptured just over four years and four months after it first broke. God's will? Absolutely. It took me just over a week and the suggestion from a dear lady at my church before it dawned on me all the things God had orchestrated to take my wife home. Just as he had planned Jane's healing he planned her departure from this world.

Several months earlier Jane complained of back pain. After visiting her doctor she was prescribed a pill to relax her muscles. The pill seemed to work to some degree. However, it made her feel so sleepy she had to sleep for twelve or more hours just to be able to function. This made it very hard, and at times impossible, for her to get out of bed in the morning. In March she returned to her doctor. This time she was prescribed a different pill, one that should not make her as drowsy. However, after taking her first pill she found it had a negative side-effect. It put her in a drunk-like state. She was unable to think clearly and even had slurred speech. Jane decided to take just half a pill during the day if she needed it. She would only take a full pill at night and then only if she was in more pain than a dose of ibuprofen could help.

On Saturday, April 15th, we worked together for an eight hour shift. After the COVID-19 shutdowns hiring new people was difficult. My company, therefore, had allowed me to hire my wife to work with me. When we got home that day we ate dinner, then I took a one hour nap. I got up and went downstairs to find Jane sitting on the couch complaining about her neck muscles hurting. She was planning a nap as well so I rubbed her neck for a while before she took some ibuprofen and when to lay down. That was at 8:30 p.m. At about 10:20 p.m. I went upstairs to check on her. She roused slightly but when I spoke to her, her response was incoherent. Thinking she must have taken one of her muscle pills I left her to continue sleeping. At 11:10 p.m. I retired for the night next to my soundly sleeping wife.

Two weeks earlier I had started volunteering for a Sunday morning ministry at my church. So for the last two Sundays I got up at 6:30 a.m., got ready and went to church, setting the alarm for Jane to get up and come in later. The Sunday of the 16th was no different. Not wanting to wake her before she needed to get up, I got ready quietly. Just before leaving I let Bailey, our greyhound and her sleep buddy, into the bedroom. He liked to sleep next to her on the bed if I left the house early.

While at church that morning I suddenly realized that I had forgotten to set the alarm for Jane. Calling her on her cell phone would be useless since I saw it downstairs plugged in for recharging. I then knew I would most likely not see her in church. If she had taken one of those muscle pills, as I expected, she would probably not wake up on her own in time to get ready for church. I left church at approximately 12:20 p.m., Jane had not shown up for church.

The week before was Easter and our local grocery store had a special offer. Customers who had earned a certain number of points could pick from either a ham, a leg of lamb or a frozen turkey breast for a discounted price. It just so happened that Jane had been saying we had not had ham for a while and she'd like to get one sometime soon. But I knew she also loved lamb. So I had asked her which one she wanted. To my surprise she said she wanted the turkey breast. So that's what I got, a frozen turkey breast, on Saturday, the day before Easter. But since it was frozen it would not be thawed for that Easter Sunday. So I put it in the refrigerator to wait the two to three days the instructions said it would take to thaw. However, a few days later, when I was off, Jane wanted to go out for the day. So the turkey breast, which was suppose to be cooked immediately after thawing, was still sitting in the fridge that Sunday. I knew I needed to cook that turkey that day or it would go bad.

I arrived home to be greeted by both of our greyhounds. Since Bailey greeted me I assumed Jane was up, somewhere in the house. I typically closed the door to the bedroom when Bailey was sleeping with her, so the fact that he was out made me believe she had gotten up. I do not know if she did get up earlier and then when back to bed or if I forgot to close the bedroom door as I had forgotten to set the alarm. But whichever the case, I did not immediately go to check on my wife. Instead I began preparing our turkey dinner. It was almost 1:00 before I climbed the steps to our bedroom. I called to Jane as I entered the room. She did not answer. I went to her and found her sleeping on her side. I shook her and said her name again but still she did not respond. I rolled her over calling to her louder. This time when she did not answer I pried open one eye, then the other one. I grabbed a nearby flashlight, turned it on and swung the light across first one eye and then the other. Her pupils were unresponsive. At 12:54 p.m. I found myself dialing 911 once again.

She was taken to our local hospital where they did an x-ray and CAT scan. Her aneurysm had re-ruptured and blood had flooded her brain. This time, however, the doctor said she was in a coma and part of her brain stem had disintegrated -- the part the controls pupil dilation. Further, the part that controlled breathing was going quickly. He did not recommend surgery. It was unlikely they would succeed in saving her life, he told me. And if they did she would be in a coma indefinitely, which if she came out of she would be little more than a vegetable and would not be able to breathe on her own. I talked to three different doctors who all concurred.

I had to make a decision and I needed to make it quick. I did not have to think long. It was a decision we had both made long ago. She would not want to live like that, I told the doctor. Then gave them permission to take the breathing tube out. I prayed, Lord, I know she would not want to live like that. If it is your will to heal her, then allow her to breathe on her own. But if not, please don't let her suffer.

The tube was taken out and she continued to breathe. I was told that Jane would not live long. Perhaps days, hours or minutes. They did not know. The decision was made to move her to a hospice center right across from the hospital. As the arrangements were made Jane's breathing seemed to come easier to her. My older brother and his wife arrived just minutes before Jane was put on a stretcher to be taken to the hospice center. The nurse told me to go with her and ride in the ambulance. She then added that sometimes they don't make it through the ride. I believe she suspected something as Jane's breathing was now barely noticeable.

The ride to the hospice center was a short one. I held Jane's hand in mine as we rode. The back of the ambulance was dark but I could still see her face, her small fingers wrapped around mine. I was glad I was there. I continued to hold her hand as she slipped into eternity. I could not have asked for a more peaceful way for the woman I loved to leave this world.

God's will? I considered the things that had happened the months and weeks before and up to the very day she passed. Jane's back pain. The prescription medication that had made her too sleepy. The new prescription that put her in a drugged-like state. When she complained of neck pain I thought it was connected with her back pain. However, it could have been her aneurysm had ruptured then. But instead of causing her to pass out it caused a slight pain she contributed to neck muscles. When I checked on her napping her speech was slurred. A fact that I contributed to her new muscle relaxer which had the same effect on her. At any other time such a thing would have been very disconcerting. My leaving the house early on Sunday mornings had started just two weeks ago. Before I would have gotten up with Jane to get ready for church. I forgot to set the alarm for her and perhaps forgot to close the bedroom door before I left. I had not forgotten to set the alarm for her or close the door before and I had done it many times when I left the house early for work. So what made me forget on that day? Then there was the extra time I took to prepare a turkey breast that should have been cooked several days before. So many things had lined-up to either keep me from suspecting something was wrong or keep me from checking on her. It was like a perfect storm of delay and deception. By the time I checked on her that Sunday afternoon it was too late. Irreversible damage had already been done. I have no doubt that God orchestrated those events to take Jane home just as sure as he orchestrated the events that led to her first ruptured aneurysm and subsequent healing. Our God is a God of purpose and planning. I do not know God's purpose in taking Jane at this time. But as I stated before, God doesn't always allow us to see His reasons for what He does. But we have to have faith that His will is always better. It may not feel like it at the moment, but if we just trust Him, His symphony, His plan, His will always works for the good. I may never know in this life what God's plan is, but I will trust Him all the same. I am thankful for the time we had together.

In the days and weeks that followed God gave me His peace. And I received it . . . most of the time. But I wish to be honest. There were a few times when I let Satan buff at me. Times when I took my eyes off the Lord and eternal things. The day after losing her I prayed the Lord would take me as well. I lamented that with no children, I had nothing to live for. The Lord gently rebuked me. "You should not have been living for her to start with. Loving her, taking care of her, yes. But not living for her." I was to be living for the Lord. He has ways of putting things in perspective. Any preacher worth his salt will tell you we are in this world to glorify God. By praise, by testimony, by witness. We are His children and His servants. Paul said, "For me to live, is Christ." (Phil. 1:21a) I pray that that may be true of me as well.

Two days later I walked outside on a beautiful sunny spring day. A light breeze made the newly forming leaves sway and glisten in the rays of sunshine. Someone had described Jane as a little ray of sunshine. Then a not so long ago thought returned to my mind. I pictured Jane standing face to face with her Savior. I suddenly began to smile. I couldn't help but think heaven must be just a little brighter today. Then I began to laugh as that beautiful day engulfed me. I thought, "She's in heaven. Heaven! There's no better place to be." Then tears of joy and happiness began to flow for my wife. I'm so glad your home.

> "What no eye has seen,
> what no ear has heard,
> and what no human mind has conceived—
> the things God has prepared for those who
> love him—"

> I Corinthians 2:9

Printed in the United States
by Baker & Taylor Publisher Services